# WALKING WITH
# MATTHEW

### BECOMING THE MAN GOD INTENDS YOU TO BE

A 30-DAY DEVOTIONAL
AND BIBLE STUDY

**FRED J. PARRY**

ILLUMIFY MEDIA GLOBAL
Littleton, Colorado

# WALKING WITH MATTHEW

Copyright © 2021 by Fred Parry

All rights reserved. No part of this book may be reproduced in any form or by any means—whether electronic, digital, mechanical, or otherwise—without permission in writing from the publisher, except by a reviewer, who may quote brief passages in a review.

All Scriptures are taken from the Holy Bible, New International Version®, NIV® Copyright © 1973, 1978, 1984, 2011 by Biblica, Inc.® Used by permission. All rights reserved worldwide.

No part of this publication may be used, reproduced, stored or transmitted without the express written permission of Fred J. Parry, 711 West Broadway, Columbia, Missouri 65203. Requests for information should be addressed to Fred Parry, 711 West Broadway, Columbia, Missouri 65203 or via email to FParry61@gmail.com

The views and opinions expressed in this book are those of the author and do not necessarily reflect the official policy or position of Illumify Media Global.

Published by
Illumify Media Global
www.IllumifyMedia.com
"Write. Publish. Market. SELL!"
Paperback ISBN: 978-0-578-81446-9
Typeset by Art Innovations (http://artinnovations.in/)
Cover design by Debbie Lewis | Interior Design by Carolyn Preul
Copy Editing: Lisa Thornton Stillwell | Technical Review: Bob Walz
Printed in the United States of America

## ACKNOWLEDGMENT:

Special thanks to my friend Bob Walz for his steadfast guidance and counsel during the writing and editing of *Walking With Matthew*. More than just encouraging me through the writing process, Bob has given me a more complete understanding of the nature of God and, for that, I will be forever indebted. Based in Lincoln, Nebraska, Bob is a staff trainer for the Navigators organization, where he has invested in thousands of young Christians for more than 40 years. Bob and his wife, Sandy, have four grown children and six grandchildren. Bob loves studying and sharing God's Word. He has a website that has many tools to help others get into the Word (www.dscplwrx.com).

For the men who have steadfastly walked by my side through my circuitous journey to a more Christ-centered life. I am forever indebted for your gifts of transparency, vulnerability, and humility; traits that had long been absent from my life. Your encouragement and wisdom have done much to enrich this second chapter of my life.

……..

*"As iron sharpens iron,
so one man sharpens another."*

**(Proverbs 27:17)**

# CONTENTS

*Introduction*   1
*How to Use This Book*   7
*Background*   11
*15 Rules of Engagement For Small Group Studies*   19

## WEEK 1

Day 1: Discipline vs. Obedience   20
Day 2: Giving Up Jealousy and Anger   22
Day 3: Producing Fruit   24
Day 4: Called to Discipleship   26
Day 5: Standing Firm in Your Faith   28

## WEEK 2

Day 1: Shining Your Light   32
Day 2: Temptation and Tolerance   34
Day 3: Keeping Score   36
Day 4: Growing Spiritually   38
Day 5: The Storms of Life   40

## WEEK 3

Day 1: God's Providence   44
Day 2: God Answers All Prayers   46
Day 3: The Authority of Jesus   48
Day 4: Mercy Trumps Sacrifice   50
Day 5: Standing Up for Christ   52

## WEEK 4

Day 1: All in for Christ ... 56
Day 2: Exchange Your Burdens ... 58
Day 3: Exposing One's Heart ... 60
Day 4: The Pitfalls of Unbelief ... 62
Day 5: Persistent Faith ... 64

## WEEK 5

Day 1: Denying Yourself ... 68
Day 2: Reckless Love of God ... 70
Day 3: Childlike Faith ... 72
Day 4: Servant Leadership ... 74
Day 5: Righteous Indignation ... 76

## WEEK 6

Day 1: Preparing The Way ... 80
Day 2: Trusting God ... 82
Day 3: The Death of Christ ... 84
Day 4: Christ is Risen ... 86
Day 5: Go. Baptize. Teach. ... 88

*Additional Resources* ... 91

For more information on using this book for a group study, please visit **www.FredParry.Life** to access study materials, handouts, and other useful information.

# INTRODUCTION

## BURIED TREASURE

*"For where your treasure is, there your heart will be also." (Matthew 6:21 NIV)*

If you're like me, you probably struggle with the constant battle of trying to determine what your priorities should be. I, too often, get distracted by the opportunities that come my way offering a new challenge, a change of scenery, or something to just break up the monotony of daily life. While I know, inherently, that I should stay focused on the task at hand, it's hard to resist the temptation of new experiences that might elevate my income, quality of life, or social status.

When it comes to prioritizing the important things in life, we often discover that we are our own worst enemies. Even something as basic as finding the appropriate balance between work responsibilities and family life is never as easy as it should be. On top of loading up our personal calendars, we do the same with our kids. Our efforts to keep them busy and out of trouble forces us into a grueling pace that only adds stress to our already complicated lives. We find ourselves stuck in a vicious cycle.

In addition to these day-to-day pressures, we burn so much of our energy and resources trying to "keep up" with the social status of our peers and neighbors. It's almost a blood sport trying to make sure that we're driving the right kind of car, making sure that our lawns are perfectly manicured and that our children are included in the social activities of the "in-crowd." It's exhausting.

Matthew's words of wisdom relating to the matters of the heart can help us put things in the right perspective. If you find yourself working in overdrive just to stay on par with the rest of the world, it's probably time to check your priorities. For most of us, the reality check is as simple as taking a look at what's in your garage, your basement, and in your closets. Our material possessions may give us temporary satisfaction, but it doesn't take long for most of us to quickly put them aside and begin yearning for the next best thing. In the end, it's important to remember that you can't take any of this "stuff" with you. We leave our worldly treasure behind as a burden for our children to either sell for a pittance in a garage sale or haul it off to the nearest landfill.

Matthew teaches us that we should instead be building up our treasures in heaven. Instead of finding satisfaction from our worldly accomplishments and trophies, our priorities should be in using our God-given treasures and talents. We often take these kinds of treasures for granted and let them go to waste. Some of us are gifted with the ability to teach, encourage, or inspire others. Others love to cook, do home improvement, or gardening. Whatever you love doing, if you're willing to do it for the benefit of others, you are honoring God with those gifts and building up your treasure in heaven. When your idea of treasure begins to align with God's, good things start happening. All of a sudden, you know your priorities are in the proper order.

There is so much wisdom to be learned from the Gospel of Matthew. Other than Revelation, no other book of the New Testament references Old Testament prophecy and teachings more than this gospel. Matthew's knitting together of old and new teachings deepens and broadens our understanding of God's Word. The more we know about God's character, the more likely we are to live out lives that are worthy of the special gifts and sacrifices made on our behalf through His Son, Jesus Christ.

As someone who actually knew Christ and walked the earth with Him, Matthew is deliberate in the wisdom he imparts on obedience, discipleship, spiritual growth, and servant leadership. My hope is that you will use this devotional to better understand your God-given gifts, assess the content of your heart, and then use those treasures to grow spiritually in the service of others. Through our actions and deeds, we can become faithful stewards of God's amazing grace, glorifying Him in all that we do.

Fred J. Parry

# HOW TO USE THIS BOOK

**W**alking with Matthew: Become The Man God Intends You To Be is designed to serve the dual purpose of being both a daily devotional and a Bible study guide for the New Testament's Gospel of Matthew. While the book is structured to be used over a six-week period, I would encourage you to use it at a pace that is most comfortable for you.

Each of the daily devotions is inspired by a passage in Matthew's gospel. From these passages, I have found themes that can guide us in our daily walk to become better Christians. From these 28 chapters, you will discover important teachings from Jesus on love, prayer, discipleship, and the dynamic relationship that existed between Jesus and God. These devotionals were written as responses from my own personal understanding of how a particular passage spoke to me. The goal of any Bible Study is to find the correct interpretation which leads to a variety of applications. That, in itself, is rightly handling the word of truth (2 Timothy 2:15).

If you're like me, you'll get a new insight or meaning each time you read one of these passages and not because the Bible's meaning has changed, but because we, as individuals, have changed since the last time we were there. We've become more aware of a different aspect of our lives, and this scripture now speaks to us in a new way. We are more teachable than we were before. The Bible takes us on where we are, and God uses His Word to lead us to greater maturity and a broader perspective. The Bible is as deep as we are and deeper still.

I would suggest approaching each devotional in prayer, asking God for clarity of mind and focus with a hope that the day's message resonates with you in some meaningful way.

**Once you've read the devotional, you'll find the following tools at the end of each reading to help you get the most meaning out of the day's message:**

- a reference to scripture outside the Gospel of Matthew that will reinforce and add context to the day's message.

- next, you'll find two short questions designed to help you apply that day's lesson to your life.

- finally, you'll find a call to contemplation which is intended as a prompt for journaling. It's an excellent opportunity to explore and record your feelings as they relate to the day's message.

In the coming pages, you'll find the complete text of the Gospel of Matthew reprinted with permission of Biblica, Inc. To gain a better understanding of the literary and cultural context of each day's passage, I would encourage you to refer to the full text each day to fully understand the contextual circumstances and events surrounding each passage.

I hope that you'll find these devotionals to be useful and relevant in your daily walk. My prayer is that the wisdom that comes from the Gospel of Matthew will guide you in your journey to lead a more fulfilling and Christ-centered life.

FJP

## MY PRAYER

*Gracious God, open our hearts and minds to receive the wisdom that comes from the Gospel of Matthew. Encourage us to be intentional in our efforts to align our priorities to serve You as we serve our fellow man. May we grow spiritually as we study the work and walk of Your Son, Jesus, when he came to this earth to save us from our sin. We pray for these things in the name of our Savior, Jesus Christ. Amen.*

# BACKGROUND

## WHO WAS MATTHEW?

Matthew was one of the original 12 disciples chosen to follow Jesus Christ. Born in Galilee, the son of Alphaeus, Matthew is identified in other Gospels as Levi, a tax collector (a.k.a. publican) who Jesus meets in Capernaum, a city located on the shores of the Sea of Galilee. Biblical scholars believe that Levi was Matthew's tribal name that he used interchangeably with his Greek name. Contracted by the Roman government to collect taxes as an agent for Herod Antipas, Matthew worked in what was, perhaps, the most despised profession of the time. It is believed that Matthew was stationed in Capernaum to collect taxes on the goods that were passing through the major trade route between Damascus and Mediterranean ports. Many of his contemporaries considered Matthew's work to be a betrayal of his Jewish heritage.

By choosing Matthew to be one of His disciples, Jesus was sending a clear message that no one would be excluded from His movement. When Matthew invites Jesus to his home for a feast that includes tax collectors and other sinners, Jesus is harshly criticized by the Pharisees for dining with the lowest rung of society. In response, Jesus answers by saying, "It is not the healthy who need a doctor, but the sick. But go and learn what this means: 'I desire mercy, not sacrifice. For I have not come to call the righteous, but sinners." (Matthew 9:12-13)

Biblical historians have relatively little information about the life of Matthew. In fact, in spite of his close relationship with Jesus, he is only mentioned in the Bible seven times. While there is some scholarly debate over the authenticity of Matthew's authorship, there has been no alternative evidence presented by any scholar that would point to another author. If Matthew was not the actual author, it is believed that he was a prominent source for much of what is presented in the gospel that bears his name. Some scholars point to the many references to money in the Gospel of Matthew as proof that is was likely written by someone who may have been a tax collector. For example, the terms gold and silver are mentioned on 28 occasions in Matthew as compared to being mentioned only four times in Luke and only once in Mark. Matthew's use of the words "forgive us our debts" in the Lord's Prayer (Matthew 6:9-13) versus the use of the phrase "forgive us our sins" in Luke's version further suggests an author with a financial background.

## THE GOSPEL OF MATTHEW

Matthew's gospel is one of four gospels included in the New Testament. The other three gospels were written by Mark, Luke, and John. The four are often referred to as "The Four Evangelists." This moniker was influenced in part by the Greek etymology of the word "evangelion" meaning "good news" or "gospel." The Gospel of Matthew is believed to have been written between 80 and 85 AD, sometime after the destruction of Jerusalem in 70 AD. While the sequence of events detailing the teachings of Jesus Christ is similar to those presented in other gospels, Matthew's writings are unique in that they bridge the teachings and prophecies of the Old Testament to events that take place during the course of Jesus' life. Though his was not the first book to be written, it is the first of the four gospels found in the New Testament, although it is believed that Mark's gospel was probably the first gospel to be written.

Through the entirety of his text, Matthew shows the correlation between the events in Jesus's life as the fulfillment of Old Testament prophecy. For example, in Matthew 2:15 when the story is told of Joseph escaping the wrath of King Herod by fleeing with the infant Jesus to Egypt, Matthew points to the prophetic words found in Hosea 11:1, "Out of Egypt, I called my son." In all, there are 15 similar references to the fulfillment of Old Testament prophecy found in the New Testament's Gospel of Matthew. Matthew, in fact, quotes the Old Testament on a greater frequency than any other gospel. The only book in the New Testament with more quotations from the Old Testament is Revelation.

Another important theme that seems to emerge from the Gospel of Matthew is that of the role of Gentiles in society and the impact they will eventually have on the growth of Christ's church. Jesus uses his encounters with the Centurion (Matthew 8:5-13) and the Canaanite woman (Matthew 15:21-28 ) as significant teaching opportunities for his disciples. Jesus is impressed by the depth of their faith and their persistence in seeking help from Jesus. He rebukes His disciples for trying to interfere in their efforts to have their loved ones healed.

## THE STRUCTURE OF THE GOSPEL OF MATTHEW

Matthew's gospel begins with an extensive genealogy tracing Jesus's ancestral lineage back to Abraham. In all, there are 42 generations listed in chronological sequence. Between Abraham and King David, there were 14 generations. From the reign of King David to the Exile in Babylon, another 14 generations had passed. Another 14 generations would pass before the birth of Jesus Christ.

To better understand the scope and context of Matthew's gospel, it is essential to understand the structure of the overall text. The Gospel of Matthew is comprised of five major discourses or themes that represent the key messages presented by the author. The first major component is found in Matthew 5-7 in what is commonly known as the Sermon on the Mount. These chapters include the Beatitudes as well as Jesus's instruction for prayer, subsequently representing what is now known as The Lord's Prayer. In this section, key Christian ideals focusing on love, humility, spirituality, and mercy are presented. The text in this section also contains important teachings on divorce, lust, and false prophets. This section gives the reader a better understanding of the relationship between God and Jesus.

The second major theme in Matthew's gospel deals with the many miracles performed by Jesus, His selection of His disciples, and the instructions He gives them. Much of chapter 10 is dedicated to how the disciples should conduct themselves as they travel from town to town spreading God's word. Included in His instructions are how and where to preach and how to deal with the opposition that will inevitably be encountered on their journeys.

The third component focuses on Jesus's relationship with His people. Through the use of parables, His teaching was quite intentional as Jesus knew that a portion of His audience might be unwilling to embrace the complex mysteries of the kingdom of heaven. To effectively make His points, Jesus employed the use of relatable worldly stories that had heavenly implications. Even though Christ was able to demonstrate God's love and mercy through His many miracles, He knew that a portion of his audience would simply be drawn in by the act of the miracle itself. Jesus wanted to set apart those who would look beyond these miracles; those who were seeking a deeper understanding of God's kingdom.

The fourth theme presented in the Gospel of Matthew focuses on the community of followers that will eventually become the Church. In chapter 18, the author reveals the instructions Jesus gave his disciples regarding their role in running the church. Jesus encourages his disciples to build the Church with a sense of humility and self-sacrifice.

The fifth and final theme in Matthew's gospel deals with a foretelling of the End Times, the anticipated destruction of the temple in Jerusalem, and the second coming of Christ. Most of the teaching on this subject was delivered to the disciples on the Mount of Olives. Readers will find strong similarities from this passage with the accounts written in Mark 13 and Luke 21. Matthew places a strong emphasis on how Jesus's followers should act as the end times approach. He warns of the suffering and sacrifice that will likely take place leading up to Christ's triumphant return.

## THE PARABLES OF CHRIST

A parable is often described as an earthly story with a heavenly meaning. Throughout His teaching, Jesus would frequently use parables when he needed to illustrate a complex thought. Parables were an effective teaching tool because the messages were typically a simple, but memorable story. The characters in the parables were relatable to the audience. Even those with no faith or any exposure to Christian teaching are familiar with these stories because many of these parables have made their way into secular culture. Today, you will hear people describe another person as "salt of the earth" or as a "good Samaritan" without having any knowledge that the roots of these terms go back to the teachings of Jesus.

Jesus used parables while preaching to large audiences that were typically a mixed group of believers and non-believers. Jesus understood best the type of teaching that would resonate with mankind. When asked why he chose to teach using parables, he said, "Though seeing, they do not see; though hearing, they do not hear or understand." (Matthew 13:13)

Throughout his gospel, Matthew shares 23 of the 33 full-fledged parables recorded in the New Testament. Of those 23 parables, 11 can only be found only in the Gospel of Matthew. Reading through the Gospels of Matthew, Luke, and Mark, you will often find many of the same parables told with only slight changes in wording; however, the universal truth and meaning is always the same. Common themes in parables usually related to growing God's kingdom, the importance of a strong prayer life, forgiveness, loss and redemption, and what it means to truly love others.

## THE GREAT COMMISSION
Perhaps, the most widely known passage in all of the Gospel of Matthew is The Great Commission (Matthew 28:16-20) where the resurrected Jesus calls his disciples to a mountaintop in Galilee and instructs them to make disciples and to baptize all nations in the name of the Father, Son, and Holy Spirit. In this passage, the eleven remaining disciples (Judas had killed himself) meet at a predetermined mountain with Jesus after the resurrection. When they see him they are caught between worship and doubt. Christ tells them of His authority and, as Lord, He commands them to go and make disciples of all nations counting on His presence with them always.

## MATTHEW'S FINAL YEARS
Matthew was among those who witnessed the ascension of Jesus into heaven. In the years that would follow, Matthew would continue his ministry work preaching the gospel to the Jewish community in Judea before traveling to the region of Ethiopia (the area south of the Caspian Sea, not Africa), Persia, Macedonia, and Syria. Roman Catholic tradition holds that Matthew died as a martyr, though there are few details to substantiate this claim. Matthew's tomb is located in the crypt of the Salerno Cathedral in southern Italy. His feast day is held annually on September 21.

# 15 RULES OF ENGAGEMENT FOR SMALL-GROUP STUDIES

1. Nothing said in the group gets discussed outside the group!
2. Be transparent. Be authentic. Be your true self.
3. Everyone needs to share, both as a speaker and a listener.
4. Encourage one another. Speak truth into each others' lives avoiding the temptation to "fix" each other.
5. Challenge each other. It's reasonable to disagree, but respect boundaries.
6. Give your darkest issues the light of day. It's incredibly liberating!
7. Be willing to be vulnerable. Take a chance and let your risk be rewarded.
8. We all have blind spots. Dare to explore what yours might be.
9. Absolutely NO gossip.
10. Embrace your mistakes. Take ownership of your weaknesses, knowing that we're all human.
11. Resist the urge to rescue others when they struggle to find the right words. Let people finish their thoughts.
12. Don't be afraid of silence. Pause and feel the weight of what has been shared.
13. Trust is our most important currency. Earn it and then be willing to extend trust to others.
14. Side conversations are not allowed; only one voice at a time.
15. When possible, find time to connect with each other outside the small group setting.

*"Blessed are those who are persecuted because of righteousness, for theirs is the kingdom of heaven."*

**(Matthew 5:10 NIV)**

# WEEK 1

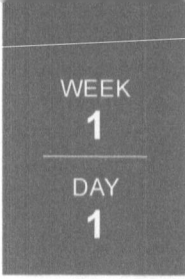

# DISCIPLINE VS. OBEDIENCE

*"Because Joseph, her husband, was faithful to the law, and yet did not want to expose her to public disgrace, he had in mind to divorce her quietly. But after he had considered this, an angel of the Lord appeared to him in a dream and said, "Joseph son of David, do not be afraid to take Mary home as your wife, because what is conceived in her is from the Holy Spirit. She will give birth to a son, and you are to give him the name Jesus, because he will save his people from their sins." (Matthew 1:19-21)*

Imagine yourself in the place of Joseph. An angel appears in a dream with some very specific instructions on how the next several months of your life are going to play out. If all goes as the angel has instructed, Joseph is going to struggle through phases of humility, pride, disgrace, and a massive reconfiguration of the life he had planned for himself and Mary. I know that I would feel angry, frustrated, and greatly inconvenienced. Not Joseph. He was so obedient to God and so faithful to Mary that there was never a moment of doubt in his mind as to what he was to do. He did exactly as the angel had instructed.

There's something written into the DNA of men that makes obedience, of any nature, seem like an insurmountable barrier. As men, it's much easier for us to master the concept and constraints of discipline over obedience because discipline is usually all about achieving something which we, ourselves, strongly desire. Discipline is most often challenged in our daily lives when our goals or behaviors conflict with the interests of others. There's always going to be someone pressuring us to eat unhealthy or skip going to the gym. With obedience, the rewards are not as always well defined. Obedience is all about following someone else's plan. When obedience is required, it seems as if we are relinquishing our cherished independence.

In Philippians 2:8, we read about the obedience of Jesus, "And being found in human form, he humbled himself by becoming obedient to the point of death, even death on a cross." Perhaps you think that it may have been easy for the omnipotent Son of God to be obedient because He knew what His future held. But what about Joseph? His faith in God and his willingness to put others first were characteristics that allowed him to follow an unconventional path. What might happen in your life if you were more willing to take a similar leap of faith, not because it was convenient but because you were obedient? When you consider the promise of God's salvation, your obedience is no longer a risky proposition.

### MY PRAYER
*God, teach me to be obedient. Give me the confidence of Joseph to seek out and embrace your plans for my life. Help me to set aside my own plans so that I may pursue a righteous relationship with You. Amen.*

### READ: JOHN 14:15-31

**QUESTION #1:** In what areas of your life should you replace discipline with obedience?

**QUESTION #2:** When you hear the term 'obedience' do you view it positively or negatively? Why or why not?

### CONTEMPLATE

Recall a time when you were completely obedient to someone other than yourself. What was the outcome? How would that experience affect your willingness to be completely obedient to God?

# GIVING UP JEALOUSY AND ANGER

*When King Herod heard this he was disturbed, and all Jerusalem with him. When he had called together all the people's chief priests and teachers of the law, he asked them where the Messiah was to be born. "In Bethlehem in Judea," they replied, "for this is what the prophet has written: "'But you, Bethlehem, in the land of Judah, are by no means least among the rulers of Judah; for out of you will come a ruler who will shepherd my people Israel." (Matthew 2:3-6)*

---

Herod knew that he was not the legitimate heir to the throne of King David and the news of the birth of the true King of Jews was unsettling to him in many ways. If Jewish people were to rally around a king of their own, Herod's power would be threatened. Herod was not alone in his displeasure. The news of God entering the world would undoubtedly challenge man's lenient attitude towards sin. Because religious leaders recognized the birth of Jesus as the fulfillment of prophecy (Micah 5:2), the pressure for Herod to take action increased and he resorted to kill all male infants under two years old. Herod's jealous rage and his strong appetite for power and control were getting the best of him.

Most of us struggle with some sort of jealousy. Some struggle with anger and rage. Most of us want to be in control of our lives. As hard as it might be to understand Herod's rationalization for his actions, it's easier for us to understand, and even relate to, the root causes of his disposition. One way to look at jealousy is to view it as our dissatisfaction with what God has given us. We choose to not be content because we believe that someone else has been given more than they deserve. Knowing that envy is a sin, we should focus our energies on being grateful for what we've been given. After all, God has given us everything we have and everything we need. To be jealous is to be disrespectful of God. The same is true of anger. Our anger is often associated with our pride.

In Hebrews 13:5, we are instructed to be content with what we've been given and to live our lives with the knowledge that God will never leave us nor forsake us. Isn't that all the assurance we should need? Herod's power was given to him by man, not by God. He had been put in power by the Romans. He was not the rightful heir to the throne, and he knew it. Surrendering control of our lives is an easy choice when we know and believe that we serve a loving God, who only wants what's best for us.

## MY PRAYER

*Heavenly Father, help me to keep my life in true perspective. When I become envious or jealous, draw my attention to the abundance of blessings in my life. When anger and rage come from my heart, humble me and enable me to set aside my pride. Keep my eyes focused on the love you have given me. Amen.*

### READ: PSALMS 10:2-11

**QUESTION #1:** How often do you experience the emotion of jealousy in your life? What are typically the circumstances? Are your emotions usually justified or proven wrong?

**QUESTION #2:** In what part of your life has pride been an issue? What are some methods you use to keep your pride in check?

### CONTEMPLATE

Write about a time in your life when you surrendered your worries to Christ. What was the outcome of that experience?

# PRODUCING FRUIT

*Produce fruit in keeping with repentance. And do not think you can say to yourselves, 'We have Abraham as our father.' I tell you that out of these stones God can raise up children for Abraham. The ax is already at the root of the trees, and every tree that does not produce good fruit will be cut down and thrown into the fire. (Matthew 3:8-10)*

---

When we meet John the Baptist, he is foretelling the coming of the Messiah and warns all that they must repent. Most of us view repentance as simply seeking forgiveness for our sins. However, true repentance is a bit more complicated. First and foremost, repentance is the means by which we can repair our relationship with God. It represents a change of mind and embracing the wholesome attitudes and behaviors that abide by God's law. More importantly, if one repents of his sin and then fails to change his behaviors and not produce works (fruits) in accordance with his new relationship with God, his repentance is nothing more than a shallow, meaningless act.

The imagery of what happens to a tree when it does not produce fruit is a powerful motivator. A barren tree is cut down and thrown into the fire. Even though it is still alive, it is worthless to the farmer. It's just using up resources for no purpose. In a like manner, a man that does not produce fruit is not advancing God's kingdom. As men, we become unfruitful when we neglect to nurture our spiritual lives or the lives of others. Our desire for independence and control over our own lives separates us from fellowship with God and hinders the Holy Spirit from doing the work that needs to be done in our hearts.

Our greed, pride, and anger deny the branches the nourishment and protection they need to be fruitful, and soon, these branches become brittle and break off, making it difficult to produce fruit again.

When we are fruitful, we are essentially allowing the Holy Spirit an "all-access pass" to our lives. In doing so, our lives can be filled with kindness, self-control, and gratitude. We seek ways to help the least among us. We feed the hungry and shelter the homeless. We are fruitful when we spread the Word of God and share the joy of Christ with others. A repentant heart is filled with the desire to start a new day that is pleasing to God. In James 2:14-26, we learn that faith without works is dead. What good is our faith, if we're not willing to sacrifice our time, resources, and heart for those who are in need?

**MY PRAYER**
*Heavenly Father, help me to recognize the opportunities I have to bear fruit. Let my repentant heart seek ways to serve others through my works and by helping them to know you more. Amen.*

### READ: JAMES 2:14-26

**QUESTION #1:** Is your life fruitful in the way that God desires? If so, describe a few of your behaviors that will bear fruit.

**QUESTION #2:** What are the things that are keeping you from being as fruitful as God wants you to be?

### CONTEMPLATE

Write about the opportunities you have to put your faith into action. In what areas of your life are you able to more consistently bear fruit?

# CALLED TO DISCIPLESHIP

*As Jesus was walking beside the Sea of Galilee, he saw two brothers, Simon called Peter and his brother Andrew. They were casting a net into the lake, for they were fishermen. "Come, follow me," Jesus said, "and I will send you out to fish for people." At once they left their nets and followed him. Going on from there, he saw two other brothers, James son of Zebedee and his brother John. They were in a boat with their father Zebedee, preparing their nets. Jesus called them, and immediately they left the boat and their father and followed him. (Matthew 4:18-22)*

---

Imagine being asked to drop everything you are doing, abandoning your plans and walking away from the livelihood that supports you and your family. When Jesus called his disciples to follow Him, he expected not a moment of hesitation. Because they were familiar with Jesus's teachings, they knew they were being called to something beyond extraordinary. Their individual decisions to follow Jesus at that very moment required not only a high degree of self-sacrifice but a willingness to take up the cross and deny themselves the comforts and stability to which they were accustomed. Can you imagine yourself making that kind of decision? How many excuses would you have to postpone or decide not to follow Jesus?

When you consider that becoming fishers of men is such a central theme in Jesus's teaching, it's interesting that the word "discipleship" never appears even once in the Bible. We know that we are called to help spread the good news of Christ. In reality, most of us feel an overwhelming sense of timidity when it comes to talking to another man about his personal faith journey and whether or not he is interested in pursuing a relationship with Jesus Christ. What God is asking us to do, pales in comparison to what he asked of his 12 disciples. God wants us to give up life as we know it (2 Cor 5:17).

For the disciples, following Jesus required a foundation of trust that He had clearly earned. The same should be true for us. In Proverbs 3:5, we are told to "trust in the Lord with all your heart and lean not on your own understanding." We must rely upon and trust in what we know about God's nature and follow His teachings. Think about the man who first asked you about your relationship with Christ. Had he been timid or hesitant, where would you be in your journey today? Accept your calling to help the unbelievers become believers in a wonderful and loving God.

### MY PRAYER
*God, teach me how to make disciples. Give me the self-assurance and passion that I need to share my love for You and guide others to You. Where there is doubt, sow confidence. Where there is fear, sow reassurance. Make me a fisher of men. Amen.*

### READ: JOHN 15:1-17

**QUESTION #1:** Why was it so important to Jesus that His disciples become fishers of men?

**QUESTION #2:** What are the barriers that keep you from making disciples? Be specific.

### CONTEMPLATE

Write about how you came to know Jesus. Who were the people who encouraged you to pursue a personal relationship with Christ? How might you emulate their behavior?

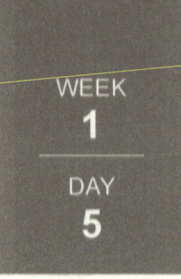

**WEEK 1 DAY 5**

# STANDING FIRM IN YOUR FAITH

*Blessed are those who are persecuted because of righteousness, for theirs is the kingdom of heaven. "Blessed are you when people insult you, persecute you and falsely say all kinds of evil against you because of me. Rejoice and be glad, because great is your reward in heaven, for in the same way, they persecuted the prophets who were before you. (Matthew 5:10-12)*

---

When Jesus was warning his disciples that they might face persecution because of their relationship with Him and for proclaiming the word of God, He wanted them to know that there would be an eternal reward for the persecution they would face faithfully. Reminding them that the prophets had also been persecuted, Jesus wanted his disciples to keep their eyes on the prize of salvation and the rewards of eternal life. Fortunately, we live in a society where Christianity is widely accepted. No one is going to stone us or rip out our toenails for sharing the good news of Jesus Christ, nor are any of us likely to be condemned for our righteousness!

In recent years, we have seen the news reports and disturbing photos of Christians being decapitated by the members of the Islamic State (ISIS). We know that persecution still exists; however, in our western civilized society, the types of persecution are of a more tame variety. There are times and places where openly sharing your faith in Christ can cause you to be marginalized by those who are unbelievers. In some situations, you may be slandered or the subject of discrimination because of your outward expressions of faith. You may feel ostracized or overlooked, but God wants you to know that there is still a reward that comes with being bold in your faith and being willing to bring others to know Christ.

# STANDING FIRM IN YOUR FAITH

In 2 Timothy 3:12, we are warned that all who desire to live a godly life in Christ will likely be persecuted. What would happen if we learned to expect this persecution and embrace it as the suffering we should endure to live a life that is pleasing to God? In fact, if we do face any type of persecution, harassment, or punishment, we should take pride in knowing that our humility and self-sacrifice are being noticed. Perhaps it's a sign that our work on behalf of the kingdom is being effective. In exchange, we can count on God's blessings and His strength to sustain us until the day we are vindicated in our actions.

## MY PRAYER

*God, give me the courage to stand firm in my faith. Let my actions rise to the level of boldness to be worthy of persecution. Help me to break out of my comfort zone by taking the fervor of my love for you to others who want to know you. I will eagerly await the vindication that will come with your return to take us home. Amen.*

### READ: 1 PETER 4:12-14

**QUESTION #1:** Has there been a time in your life where you felt marginalized or discriminated against because of your outward faith in Christ?

**QUESTION #2:** What are the things that stand between your existing life and a life of righteousness?

### CONTEMPLATE

Write about a time when you were teased or ridiculed because of your passion for a sports team, favorite music or a relationship with another person. How did you respond? Would you respond the same way if someone criticized your passion for Christ?

*"You are the light of the world.
A town built on a hill cannot be hidden."*

**(Matthew 5:14 NIV)**

# WEEK 2

# SHINING YOUR LIGHT

*"You are the light of the world. A town built on a hill cannot be hidden. Neither do people light a lamp and put it under a bowl. Instead, they put it on its stand, and it gives light to everyone in the house. In the same way, let your light shine before others, that they may see your good deeds and glorify your Father in heaven. (Matthew 5:14-16)*

Jesus told his disciples that if they would live for Him, they would glow like lamps for all to see what Christ was like. He, in turn, warned them that leading lives of passivity and fear would be the equivalent of hiding the light of Jesus. When we choose to go along to get along with the crowd instead of standing up and doing the right thing, we hide the light. When we are passive and unprincipled, we allow ourselves, and others, to slip into darkness. When we give in to gratification of the flesh or allow our tongues to spread the poison of harmful words, we are succumbing to sin and dulling the shine of God's light to those around us. Our light dims further when we avoid the truth or simply deny others the good news of Jesus.

As men, we find ourselves instinctively gravitating toward dark places. Driven by greed or lust or sloth, we take refuge in vices like pornography or material possessions that provide a temporary distraction from our pain. We too often find comfort in the things of this world and that's exactly where the devil wants us. We should, instead, be shining light into the dark places in our world. When the desires of our flesh outweigh the calling of the Spirit, we find ourselves moving down a path of certain destruction. We often move towards isolation and that creates a fertile ground for Satan, who has a mission to destroy our hearts and separate us from God.

# SHINING YOUR LIGHT

In Galatians 5:19-21, the apostle Paul warns us that our acts of sexual immorality, idolatry, and selfish ambition will keep us from inheriting the kingdom of God. But Matthew reminds us that our new identity is to stand up, be assertive and live out our calling to be the salt of the earth. This new culture of the kingdom is counter-cultural. While others are pursuing physical pleasures and self-centered gain, we will have to resist temptation and demonstrate what it's like to live with God's light. We are called to give praise and encouragement to others, always putting their needs before our own. Giving light to everyone in the house will require us to do what is right versus what feels good. We must then overcome our fear of being judged or criticized for simply doing the right thing. If our intentions are pure, our spiritual maturity will be rewarded in immeasurable ways.

## MY PRAYER

*God, give me the courage to be bold in my faith and to stand up to the things that threaten to pull myself and others into the darkness. Let me be that city on a hill, giving light to everyone in the world around me. Amen.*

## READ: GALATIANS 5:19-21

**QUESTION #1:** Recall a time when you felt compelled to stand up and do the right thing, but instead, chose to be passive.

**QUESTION #2:** What steps can you take to keep others from being pulled into the darkness?

## CONTEMPLATE

Write about the things you can do in your daily routine to become a light for others. What obstacles must you overcome to do that?

# TEMPTATION AND TOLERANCE

*If your right eye causes you to stumble, gouge it out and throw it away. It is better for you to lose one part of your body than for your whole body to be thrown into hell. And if your right-hand causes you to stumble, cut it off and throw it away. It is better for you to lose one part of your body than for your whole body to go into hell. (Matthew 5:29-30)*

If you're not one of those guys who struggles with sin and temptation, there's an excellent chance that you're either in deep denial or your heart has flat lined and you are among the walking dead. When Jesus suggests gouging out your eye if what you see is causing temptation, He is, of course, speaking figuratively; however, it shows the extreme importance of eliminating the things in our lives that lead to sin. To overcome sin and temptation, we have to focus our attention on the things that cause us to sin and work to eliminate those things from our lives. If watching television or getting on the internet alone at night tempts you to view pornography, you need to stop doing those things alone at night. If drinking more than three beers causes you to be flirtatious, limit yourself to only two beers.

We must be mindful that we have an enemy that is attempting to destroy us. To be effective, the enemy wants us to think that we're all alone in our struggles. When we believe this, we cave in to the circumstances that create fertile ground for sinful behavior. One of the challenges in fighting off sin is society's ever-increasing tolerance for sinful behavior. In fact, the word "tolerance" itself has become a buzzword in a culture that seems to constantly be pressuring us to compromise our convictions so that others can sin as they wish with no fear of being judged or having consequences for their behavior. Jesus was tolerant in many ways when it came to loving others; however, He was completely intolerant of hypocrisy, self-centered behavior, and sin. Jesus hates sin.

Later in Matthew 7:14, we will learn that Jesus wants us to take a more difficult, narrow path, which requires us to be more disciplined and obedient in our daily lives. To protect us along the way, He has equipped us with spiritual armor and the gift of the Holy Spirit to fend off the attacks of our enemy. In following the example of Christ, we need to stand firm in our convictions and refuse modern society's push to make us tolerant of sin. We must remember that Jesus was so intolerant of sin that He died on a cross to wipe away our sin.

### MY PRAYER

*Heavenly Father, lead me away from the sin and temptation that is present in my life and in my deepest thoughts. Let me wrap myself in the spiritual armor with which you have equipped me. Let me feel the presence of the Holy Spirit when the enemy attacks. Give me the boldness and strength I need to resist. I pray for these things in the name of your Son, Jesus. Amen.*

### READ: JAMES 1:12-16

**QUESTION #1:** What are the circumstances or situations that make you susceptible to sin?

**QUESTION #2:** What does "taking the narrow path" look like in your life?

### CONTEMPLATE

Write about the sin in your life. What are some of the ways you can successfully resist the temptation that causes this sin? What are the obstacles and barriers preventing you from eliminating this sin?

# KEEPING SCORE

*"You have heard that it was said, 'Eye for eye, and tooth for tooth.' But I tell you, do not resist an evil person. If anyone slaps you on the right cheek, turn to them the other cheek also. And if anyone wants to sue you and take your shirt, hand over your coat as well. If anyone forces you to go one mile, go with them two miles. Give to the one who asks you, and do not turn away from the one who wants to borrow from you. (Matthew 5:38-42)*

Are you someone who keeps score? You're not alone. We happen to live in a 'quid pro quo' world where most of us have learned from a very early age that if you scratch someone else's back, sooner or later, they're going to come back around and scratch your back. That's just the way the world works, right? Well, that's not the way God's kingdom works. When we place conditions on our acts of kindness, we are denying God's request that we give cheerfully and love others freely, expecting absolutely nothing in return. God wants us to be selfless, valuing others above ourselves.

In a like manner, we learn in 1 Peter 3:9 that we are not to repay evil with evil. In fact, Jesus instructs us to repay an evil act with a blessing in return. Jesus speaks of the Old Testament call to take an eye for an eye as a call to seek fair justice and not revenge greater than the offense. When we seek revenge or retaliation, even when we have clearly been wronged, we are sending a signal that we believe we, ourselves, are self-righteous. In the kingdom of Christ the new way is that we must forgive because we have been forgiven. God sent his only son to die for our sinfulness and now our ransom has been paid in full. He forgave us, and so we, too, shall forgive others.

Ultimately, God is the final judge and arbiter on every sin that is either committed by us or against us. It is not our place to exact revenge or to play the role of victim. Sin against another person is ultimately a sin against God. Instead, we should offer a blessing to those we believe have hurt us. While it may be instinctual to keep score, it's not the way God wants us to live. We are to be merciful and understanding, no matter how severe the offense. It's a tall order to live this way, but God will give you the courage and strength you need to forgive others. You've heard the saying "forgive and forget." Forgetting is hard to do unless every time another's sin against you comes up in your heart you forgive.

## MY PRAYER

*God, teach me to forgive my debtors as you have forgiven my debts and transgressions. Give me the strength and courage to love in the unconditional way you have loved me. Let me be ever mindful that you are the ultimate judge and let me learn from the grace and mercy that you extend so freely. Amen.*

### READ: LUKE 6:36-38

**QUESTION #1:** How difficult is it for you to extend a blessing to someone who has sinned against you? Explain.

**QUESTION #2:** Do you have "quid pro quo" relationships with others? How could you modify your own expectations of these relationships?

### CONTEMPLATE

Write about a time in your life when you failed to extend forgiveness to someone whom you believe sinned against you. What is the current status of that relationship?

**WEEK 2 DAY 4**

# GROWING SPIRITUALLY

*If you love those who love you, what reward will you get? Are not even the tax collectors doing that? And if you greet only your own people, what are you doing more than others? Do not even pagans do that? Be perfect, therefore, as your heavenly Father is perfect. (Matthew 5:46-48)*

---

When I decided to give my life to Christ, it was a big decision. My expectation was that I would instantaneously be a better person, less distracted by all forms of temptation and cured of my propensity to frequently use colorful language. Little did I know that I would spend the rest of my life maturing as a Christian, taking two steps forward and always at least one step back. I underestimated both the process and the effort that would be required. Matthew reminds us that God wants us to continue to grow as Christians, maturing spiritually in all aspects of our lives. In fact, God desires that we strive to be perfected in Christ, following the example set by Christ. Most of us have been conditioned by this world to settle for something a little less than perfect; however, God is still there, cheering us on to have a bold finish.

We need to somehow find a way to separate ourselves from the rest of the world's sinful values. We must become devoted to God's values and not our own. One of the ways to mature as a Christian is to take every opportunity to pass along the good news of God's word. In a more practical effort, we can simply stop focusing on the sin of others and shift our attention inward to our sin. We can do a better job of controlling our tongues and become better listeners. When we feel a calling to grow in our faith, we ultimately learn to become more dependent on Christ rather than on our ways. Our spiritual growth will begin to yield a more authentic love for others, a stronger sense of self-control, and a new level of perseverance through life's more challenging times.

In 1 Corinthians 13:11, Paul reminds us that when we were children, we talked, thought, and reasoned like children. When we became men, we put our childish ways behind us. Our spiritual journey should be the same. God's expectations of us also changes as we grow in years. He wants us to rise above the mediocrity that has defined our journeys thus far. While it's not likely that any of us can become flawless, God wants us to rise when we fall and walk again in obedience motivated by His grace.

### MY PRAYER
*God, help me to grow as a Christian. Help me to put aside my childish and immature ways and push myself to know You better by investing my time in Your Word and following the example set by Your Son, Jesus. Draw me close to you as I pursue a life that is more pleasing to You. Amen.*

### READ: 1 CORINTHIANS 3:1-4

**QUESTION #1:** Which of your daily activities are likely to support your spiritual growth?

**QUESTION #2:** What practices can you add to your daily routine that will make you more spiritually mature?

### CONTEMPLATE

Think about a person you know who has grown in his/her spiritual maturity. Write about the changes you've noticed in them and the ways in which they are now different. Can you see these kinds of changes ever taking place in yourself? Why or why not?

# THE STORMS OF LIFE

*"Therefore everyone who hears these words of mine and puts them into practice is like a wise man who built his house on the rock. The rain came down, the streams rose, and the winds blew and beat against that house; yet it did not fall, because it had its foundation on the rock. But everyone who hears these words of mine and does not put them into practice is like a foolish man who built his house on sand. The rain came down, the streams rose, and the winds blew and beat against that house, and it fell with a great crash." (Matthew 7:24-27)*

Every one of us will encounter unexpected storms in our life. How those storms affect us will likely depend on how we've equipped ourselves, spiritually. Like an athlete who experiences an injury, the amount of conditioning this athlete has endured over time will largely determine how disruptive the injury becomes. The amount of strength and agility training in that athlete's career is analogous to the spiritual conditioning we do as Christians in anticipation of challenging times. In spite of our best intentions, life inevitably happens.

Like the man who built his house on rock, building a solid foundation in our Christian lives requires us to make appropriate choices along the journey. A Christ-centered life is not a passive life. Showing up at church or reading the Bible doesn't give you the type of conditioning you need to weather life's storms. It's not just hearing the Word of God, it's about living it out in our everyday lives. Building on rock requires you to act on your faith and live a righteous life, avoiding sin of any kind. There will be times where you will have to risk friendships and draw unwanted attention to yourself because you stood up for what is right, and not for what simply feels good. A life built on rock seems more complicated and demanding than that of a life built on sand, that is, until the storm comes.

The world is filled with things that seem to be designed to turn our minds and hearts away from godly living. Ultimately, it comes down to whether or not we're willing to be obedient to God. In the end, you'll discover that it's much easier to overcome financial struggles, lustful temptation, or personal losses when your life is structured in a deep accordance with God. You can seek wisdom from God for all aspects of your life. This wisdom will give you strength and a solid foundation on which to build your life. All other ground is sinking sand.

## MY PRAYER
*God, give me the wisdom to recognize that my life may not be built on a solid foundation. Help me to recognize the behaviors that are sand and those which are granite. Prepare me for life's storms so that I may stand firm in the knowledge that I have acted on my faith and dedicated my life as one that is pleasing to You. Amen.*

### READ: JAMES 1:22-27

**QUESTION #1:** What activities in your life weaken the foundation of your relationship with God?

**QUESTION #2:** What activities strengthen this foundation?

### CONTEMPLATE

Write about a time in your life when you encountered a storm that might have threatened the very foundation of your life. How did you react? What was the ultimate outcome?

*"It is not the healthy who need a doctor, but the sick. But go and learn what this means: 'I desire mercy, not sacrifice.' For I have not come to call the righteous, but sinners."*

**(Matthew 9:12-13 NIV)**

# WEEK 3

# GOD'S PROVIDENCE

*"But seek first his kingdom and his righteousness, and all these things will be given to you as well. Therefore do not worry about tomorrow, for tomorrow will worry about itself. Each day has enough trouble of its own." (Matthew 6:33-34)*

As men, we tend to be planners by nature. In every aspect of our lives, we like to have a game plan, whether it involves our personal finances, retirement plans, next year's family vacation, or our next new car. God supports our planning efforts as long as those plans are not self-centered. You can usually tell if a plan is self-centered if it causes you worry. Worrying about tomorrow's needs, plans, and uncertainties reveal a lack of trust in God's plans for our lives. If you have anxiety and worry is a common characteristic in your life, you're not alone; however, know that God has plans for you to prosper and thrive. You simply have to put your trust in God, where it belongs.

In 1 Peter 5:7, we are told to cast all of our worries and anxieties on God because He cares for us. The good news is that we have a Savior who will give us strength and positive energy in times of worry and doubt. Because we can trust in God's guidance in all things, there's no need to fret or chew our fingernails and endure the damage that stress does to our bodies. We can be free from all of this by simply submitting to and trusting in God. There are so many things that compete for our attention and distract us from God. Worry should no longer be one of those distractions.

The bottom line here is that God always provides. We often read of God's providence in scripture. What does providence mean? It means

# GOD'S PROVIDENCE

God's actions to make provision for the future. God always provides and if you have any doubt about that fact, look into the rearview mirror of your life. There has never been a time when God has forsaken you. He is always on watch and He will always be the pilot in control at the wheel of our lives. God is sufficient in every way and what He has given us is and will always be sufficient. Knowing this, we can put off tomorrow's anxiety until tomorrow knowing that today's troubles are enough to keep us busy. Trust in God and make Him the focus of your life. Everything else will fall into place.

### MY PRAYER

*Heavenly Father, remind me when I am troubled that your grace and mercy are always sufficient. When I am in doubt and despair, remind me of Your providence. When I look towards tomorrow, steer my thoughts to the ways that I might serve You and Your glorious kingdom today. Amen.*

### READ: ROMANS 10:11-14

**QUESTION #1:** What is meant by the words in today's passage that read "all these things will be given to you?"

**QUESTION #2:** What are some of the things that men most commonly worry about?

### CONTEMPLATE

Recall a time in your life when you were overwhelmed with worry or fear. How would putting your worries in God's hands have changed the way you felt? How might it have affected the outcome?

# GOD ANSWERS ALL PRAYER

*"Ask and it will be given to you; seek and you will find; knock and the door will be opened to you. For everyone who asks receives; the one who seeks finds; and to the one who knocks, the door will be opened. "Which of you, if your son asks for bread, will give him a stone? Or if he asks for a fish, will give him a snake?" (Matthew 7: 7-10)*

---

Ask. Seek. Knock. With those three words, Jesus summed up everything his disciples would need to know about praying to God. The same message is true for you and me. When we need something, we should ask God for what we need. As we are already aware, God knows exactly what we need but if we want God's will to be done on this earth, we have to be steadfast in making sure that our prayer life is not a self-centered affair. We must seek God with all of our hearts and then ask him to open doors in our life. God will open those doors by answering our genuine prayers in some form or fashion. He may not do it on our timeline or in exactly the way we asked; however, we can count on God answering our prayers.

Much has been written on the manner and method in which we should pray. By adding structure to our prayers, we can seek fellowship with God in a whole new way. Jesus tells us to begin our prayers by expressing our adoration for God, giving Him thanks for all that He has done in our lives. We are then to confess our sins and seek forgiveness, but not until we have first sought reconciliation with those we've sinned against. Once we've sought reconciliation and asked for God's forgiveness, we are then to offer prayers on behalf of others. When these prayers are offered to God in the name of his Son, Jesus, God hears our prayers. Praying in Jesus's name is not just a way to end our prayers but an acknowledgement that our privilege to ask Father God for anything comes from our relationship with His Son.

God wants us to ask Him for what we desire instead of just relying on our own ambitions. If we don't get what we desire, it's most often because we simply haven't asked God. We have not because we ask not. When we do ask, we must ask fervently and in faith. Our prayers should be persistent and frequent. We should expect an answer from God. The answer will come. Out of his immense love for us, he will give us bread when we ask for bread and fish when we ask for fish. Our God is a loving God. We will find Him when we seek Him with all our heart (Jeremiah 29:13).

## MY PRAYER

*God, let me seek you with all of my heart. Let my prayer life be fervent and persistent as I seek ways to let Your will be done on this earth. Let me pray for others first and use my prayers to build fellowship with You. Let all my prayers be genuine, selfless and said in the name of your Son and my Savior, Jesus Christ. Amen.*

### READ: JAMES 4:2-3

**QUESTION #1:** Do you believe that God answers all prayers? Why or why not?

**QUESTION #2:** Based on today's reading, what do you need to change about your prayer life?

### CONTEMPLATE

Write about a time in your life when it seemed like God did not answer your prayer. What was the eventual outcome? How did God respond?

WEEK 3
DAY 3

# THE AUTHORITY OF JESUS

*When Jesus had entered Capernaum, a Centurion came to him, asking for help. "Lord," he said, "my servant lies at home paralyzed, suffering terribly." Jesus said to him, "Shall I come and heal him?" The centurion replied, "Lord, I do not deserve to have you come under my roof. But just say the word, and my servant will be healed. (Matthew 8:5-8)*

---

"Just say the word and my servant will be healed." No matter how you read those words, you instantly know that the Centurion had immense faith in Jesus and His ability to heal someone from miles away. The Centurion considered himself unworthy of even speaking to Jesus so he first approached a group of Jewish elders asking them to be his intermediaries. The dynamics here are interesting. Jewish tradition dictated that Gentiles were considered an unwashed class of people. The additional fact that this Centurion had been stationed in Palestine for the purpose of making sure Jews remained subject to the Emperor's rule simply added to the complexity of the situation. But yet, the Centurion had won the favor of Jewish elders.

Even though the Centurion had authority over 100 Roman soldiers and had great earthly power, he was respectful and subservient to Jesus. When Jesus heard his words, he marveled at the Centurion's humility and faith. Before Him was a Roman soldier, a Gentile who was looked down upon and despised because of his ethnicity and his position in life. Jesus was moved by the condition of the Centurion's heart and had no concern for anything else. The Centurion knew that Jesus, too, would regard his servant to be just as important as a king. By performing a miracle at the Centurion's request, Jesus sent a message that multitudes of Gentiles would also have their eternal home in God's kingdom.

This story of the Centurion is filled with many lessons that not only help us gain a better understanding of our Savior but also illustrate how we should live our Christian lives. We learn from this passage that the spoken word of Jesus has an authority like none other. There's also a lesson on loving one's enemies. God's acceptance and blessing of the Gentiles sends a powerful message that there's room in our hearts to love those who are different from us. Finally, more than just the power to heal from a distance, Jesus demonstrated the omnipresence of God, a power that transcends time and space proving that our God can be with every one of us in every moment of our lives. Knowing this should change the way we live our lives.

### MY PRAYER
*God, give me the faith and humility of the Roman soldier. Let me live a life that is worthy of Your love knowing that You are by my side every moment of the day. Give me the courage to surrender my earthly authority so that I can surrender to Your authority. I pray for this in the name of your Son, Jesus Christ. Amen.*

### READ: LUKE 7:1-10

**QUESTION #1:** How does your faith differ from that of the Centurion?

**QUESTION #2:** What lessons can you learn from the Centurion that could be applied to your life?

### CONTEMPLATE

Write about a time when you were weak in your faith while facing what seemed like an insurmountable challenge. What were the circumstances? What was the outcome?

WEEK 3
DAY 4

# MERCY TRUMPS RELIGION

*"As Jesus went on from there, he saw a man named Matthew sitting at the tax collector's booth. "Follow me," he told him, and Matthew got up and followed him. While Jesus was having dinner at Matthew's house, many tax collectors and sinners came and ate with him and his disciples. When the Pharisees saw this, they asked his disciples, "Why does your teacher eat with tax collectors and sinners?" On hearing this, Jesus said, "It is not the healthy who need a doctor, but the sick. But go and learn what this means: 'I desire mercy, not sacrifice.' For I have not come to call the righteous, but sinners." (Matthew 9:9-13)*

---

For many of us, much of what shaped our views on religion and God had a lot to do with our childhood experiences with church-goers who came across as self-righteous, judgmental, and condescending. When we saw these "Christians" engaging in behavior that seemed inconsistent with the views they espoused, it left a bad taste in our mouths. In this passage, we see that Jesus had the same type of experience with the Pharisees. While they knew God's law and could preach it by chapter and verse, they had little mercy or compassion for the weak and vulnerable or for those who had lived sinful lives. The Pharisees seemed to have little interest in the most important elements of God's law... justice, mercy, and faith.

The notion that Jesus would dine at the home of Matthew with other tax collectors, sinners, and idolaters greatly offended the Pharisees. This was of no concern to Jesus. After all, He had come to this earth to call sinners. Jesus was "inclusive" long before being "inclusive" was politically correct. Jesus saw goodness where others only saw despicable outcasts. At great personal risk, which would eventually cost him his life, Jesus focused his energies and attention on saving people who did not seem worth saving.

In the end, we need to be able to distinguish the difference between mercy and sacrifice. The prophet Hosea prescribed that sacrifice requires much less of us than mercy. Sacrifice can become routine requiring very little from the heart whereas mercy requires us to build Christ-centered relationships. Sacrifice shows our devotion to religion but mercy involves loving our neighbors and serving the least among us. Showing compassion to the most undesirable or most sinful people in our community speaks volumes about the character of our hearts.

### MY PRAYER
*Father God, help me to set aside my prejudice and bias against those I once considered unworthy of my love or Yours. Help me to see beyond a person's history and focus instead on his future. Let me see the goodness in all whom I meet. I pray for these things in the name of your Son, Jesus Christ. Amen.*

### READ: HOSEA 6:1-11

**QUESTION #1:** What lessons can we apply to our lives from Jesus regarding his choice of dinner companions at Matthew's house?

**QUESTION #2:** What is the meaning of the words in today's passage, "I desire mercy, not sacrifice?"

### CONTEMPLATE

Write about the ways in which you can be more merciful to those outside your circle of influence. What will it take to push you outside your comfort zone?

**WEEK 3 — DAY 5**

# STANDING UP FOR CHRIST

*"The student is not above the teacher, nor a servant above his master. It is enough for students to be like their teachers, and servants like their masters. If the head of the house has been called Beelzebul, how much more the members of his household! (Matthew 10:24-25)*

Have you ever had someone accuse you of something that was nothing more than an outright lie? Did you feel like your reputation had been irreparably damaged? If so, you're not alone. The world is full of men (and women) who will fabricate misinformation about others, all in an effort to make themselves look better. As Jesus was giving instructions to his disciples about what their ministries would look like in the days and months to come, He wanted to make it perfectly clear that they would be under attack. If the Pharisees were bold enough to compare Jesus to Satan (Beelzebul), there was no telling what the true followers and disciples of Jesus would face in the months and days ahead. Jesus knew that there would be no limits to the types of persecution his disciples would face.

Jesus told his disciples to stand firm in their convictions. The only thing these disciples had to lose, after all, was their lives. Sounds pretty radical, right? His point was that no man could take away their guarantee of the eternal life they had earned with God. The disciples would face horrific circumstances and all but one of them would die as martyrs. More than 2,000 years later, Christians are still facing extreme persecution. The images of Islamic State (ISIS) fighters decapitating Christians remind us that some are still giving their lives by standing firm for Jesus.

Pastor John Piper once wrote, "Jesus had the love to suffer for me, that I might have the faith to suffer with Him." There's no doubt regarding the amount of love Jesus has for us. After all, he saved all of us from the penalty of our sins by dying for us on the cross. I would imagine that most of the people reading this devotional haven't been asked to do much suffering as a result of their relationship with Christ. Sadly, most of us feel inconvenienced or uncomfortable by the simple request that we love our neighbors and take care of those who are the least among us. This is how Jesus lived and we are called to be like our master.

## MY PRAYER

*God, teach me to be bold in my faith. Let me be known as a follower of Christ by my actions rather than my claims. Let me take responsibility for my relationship with Christ. Encourage me to stand firm should I ever have the honor of being attacked because of my faith in You. I pray for these things in the name of Your Son, Jesus Christ. Amen.*

### READ: TIMOTHY 3:10-17

**QUESTION #1:** How can you become bolder in your faith, without speaking a word?

**QUESTION #2:** How far are you willing to go in defending your relationship with Christ?

### CONTEMPLATE

Write about a time in your life when your faith in Christ led to some form of suffering or inconvenience. How did this experience affect your conviction toward Christ?

*"Come to me, all you who are weary and burdened, and I will give you rest."*

**(Matthew 11:28 NIV)**

# WEEK 4

**WEEK 4 — DAY 1**

# ALL IN FOR CHRIST

*"Anyone who loves their father or mother more than me is not worthy of me; anyone who loves their son or daughter more than me is not worthy of me. Whoever does not take up their cross and follow me is not worthy of me. Whoever finds their life will lose it, and whoever loses their life for my sake will find it. (Matthew 10:37-39)*

---

Have you ever been part of a team where your coach or boss demanded total commitment to a cause or team goal? Maybe you've worked for someone who asked for a 150% effort? Maybe you served in the military during a time of active combat and one of your commanders expected you to be willing to give up your life to advance the cause. That's the proposition that Jesus was presenting to his followers. Jesus wants His followers to be willing to 'take up the cross' in the little and big decisions of our lives, even giving up our lives if necessary if that's what it takes to grow the kingdom of God.

At one time or another, most of us have been advised by well-meaning people to put our families first. However, our mission for Christ requires us to ignore the societal values and priorities of our sinful world. While our families are extremely important, we are called to put God first in all that we do. When my sons would return home every summer from a Christian sports camp, they had the message stamped into their brains to put "God first, others second and myself third." Of course, that message lasted until we started to make our way home from camp when one of them would inevitably yell, "Shotgun!" on the way to the car.

God's demand to be first in our lives is not an act of arrogance on His part, but rather an act of love. He knows that if we love Him first our lives will go the way He designed life to be. He cannot give us the fulfillment of His promises until He is first the master of the premises. His message has always been consistent. Throughout the gospels, Jesus was repeatedly asked about the greatest of the Ten Commandments. The answer never changed. "Love God with all heart and all your might and all your strength; and love your neighbor as yourself." We must remember that all love comes from God and if He's not first, we likely won't have the love we need to love ourselves or our neighbors. God loved us first and He doubled down when He gave us his only Son. When this message sinks in, it's much easier for us to let go, and let God be first in our lives.

### MY PRAYER

*Heavenly Father, help me to clear my mind of the misplaced priorities, values, and morals of this sinful world. Let me keep my eyes and my heart on You. Let me put You at the top of my "To Do" list and let my first breath in the morning exalt Your holy name. Break me free from the bondage of this sinful world. I pray for these things in the name of your Son, Jesus Christ. Amen.*

### READ: COLOSSIANS 3:1-4

**QUESTION #1:** How did you react the last time someone asked you to give more than a 100% effort?

**QUESTION #2:** What are the obstacles preventing you from putting God before your family?

### CONTEMPLATE

Write about an experience in your life when you were completely committed to accomplishing a major goal. What would it take for you to apply that same level of obedience and discipline to serving God?

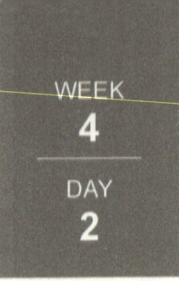

# EXCHANGE YOUR BURDENS

*"Come to me, all you who are weary and burdened, and I will give you rest. Take my yoke upon you and learn from me, for I am gentle and humble in heart, and you will find rest for your souls. For my yoke is easy and my burden is light." (Matthew 11:28-30)*

---

Perhaps you might remember the old Westerns we used to watch on television that would usually feature a team of oxen or draft horses pulling a cart or a plow? The wooden beam that joined these two animals together was called a yoke. The yoke was designed to help two or more animals share the burden of pulling a heavy load. In this passage Jesus offers us a chance to share our burdens and weariness with Him. No matter how large the load or how heavy the burden, Jesus is offering a unique partnership with us where He will help us through our weariness, problems, and anxieties by shouldering some of the burden. Jesus may not always solve our problems, but he always sees us through our problems.

Make no mistake, Jesus is not offering us a free ride. There's still plenty of work that we must do and we've learned that being a true follower of Jesus requires sacrifice, mercy, and an unrelenting desire to serve God by serving others. We've learned that partnering with Jesus may subject us to brutal persecution, but attempting to navigate life's challenges without Jesus is a fool's errand. In Proverbs 3:5-6 we learn that when we are troubled, we should trust in the Lord with all our heart and not rely on our own instincts when making decisions. When we submit to God and seek His advice, He will guide and protect us in our decision making.

Unfortunately, there's no magic pill to get us through our tough times; however, Jesus gives us something that we desperately need…hope.

Without hope, we are doomed in almost everything we do. Jesus is the answer to the questions our hearts are asking. He is where we should start, the middle, and where we should always end up. Jesus just doesn't tell us to "cheer up" or to "pick ourselves up by the bootstraps." Instead, He shows us the way by fulfilling His promise to us when we agree to share our burdens with Him. Jesus invites all of us to come to Him, abide in Him, and then find rest for our souls. Following Jesus instead of pursuing our own pathways will introduce us to a work that we will find compelling and meaningful. Jesus will exchange our burdens for a new life filled with purpose and passion. Believe. Abide. Follow. Rest.

## MY PRAYER

*God, give me the wisdom to understand that my burdens are best handled when I share them with you. Lead me to a life where I can believe and abide in You long before trouble comes my way. Let me trust in You, God, with all my heart. I pray for these things in the name of Your Son, Jesus Christ. Amen.*

### READ: PSALMS 62:5-7

**QUESTION #1:** What are the burdens in your life that you should be sharing with Jesus?

**QUESTION #2:** What are the obstacles keeping you from placing your complete trust in Jesus?

### CONTEMPLATE

Write about the person on this earth whom you trust more than any other. In what ways can placing your trust in God compare to trusting this person?

**WEEK 4 DAY 3**

# EXPOSING ONE'S HEART

*"Make a tree good and its fruit will be good, or make a tree bad and its fruit will be bad, for a tree is recognized by its fruit. You brood of vipers, how can you who are evil say anything good? For the mouth speaks what the heart is full of. A good man brings good things out of the good stored up in him, and an evil man brings evil things out of the evil stored up in him. But I tell you that everyone will have to give account on the day of judgment for every empty word they have spoken. For by your words you will be acquitted, and by your words you will be condemned." (Matthew 12:33-37)*

In the context of this passage, Jesus has just healed a deaf and dumb man and cast the evil spirits out of his body. The man regained his vision and his ability to speak. When the crowds witnessed this miracle, many began to believe that Jesus was indeed the Son of David, their long-awaited Messiah. Feeling threatened by Jesus' growing credibility and influence, the Pharisees and Scribes began telling the crowds that Jesus was only doing Satan's work. Jesus rebuked them and pointed out that their evil words were a reflection of the evil that existed in their hearts. By attributing the work of the Holy Spirit to Satan the Pharisees and Scribes had blasphemed Him; the only sin that cannot be forgiven.

In confronting the Pharisees, Jesus uses a parable to make the case that only a good tree can produce good fruit and that bad fruit can only come from a bad tree. Jesus was making the point that His good deeds, the miracles he had performed, were proof that He was good and not evil. He further pointed out that the evil words and blasphemy coming from their mouths were coming from evil hearts. The same is true for us. We are judged by our words because they reveal the condition of our hearts.

# EXPOSING ONE'S HEART

As men, most of us struggle with the temptation to curse and use foul language, most commonly in the company of other men. We may defend our bad language by making the case that "it's just locker room talk" or "just messing around with the guys" but, unfortunately, our words are exposing our wounded hearts and the weaknesses of our character. Our attempts to clean up our language will be useless until we allow the Holy Spirit to fill our hearts with new attitudes and motivations. When that happens, our speech will be cleansed at the core of our brokenness. By our words our hearts will be known.

## MY PRAYER
*God, allow the Holy Spirit to work in my heart so that it might be cleansed and replenished with only that which is pure. Help me to be consistent, matching my words and actions with that which is in my heart. Let me use my words to build up rather than destroy. I pray for these things in the name of your Son, Jesus Christ. Amen.*

### READ: JAMES 3:1-12

**QUESTION #1:** If the content of our hearts is reflected by the words we use, what do your words, in the presence of other men, reveal about your heart?

**QUESTION #2:** Recall a time when your words had a negative impact on a friend or loved one. How did you feel once you realized the impact of your words?

### CONTEMPLATE

Write a prayer asking God to cleanse your heart and fill it with new motivations and attitudes. Make it personal, being as specific as possible.

# THE PITFALLS OF UNBELIEF

*"When Jesus had finished these parables, he moved on from there. Coming to his hometown, he began teaching the people in their synagogue, and they were amazed. "Where did this man get this wisdom and these miraculous powers?" they asked. "Isn't this the carpenter's son? Isn't his mother's name Mary, and aren't his brothers James, Joseph, Simon and Judas? Aren't all his sisters with us? Where then did this man get all these things?" And they took offense at him. But Jesus said to them, "A prophet is not without honor except in his own town and in his own home." And he did not do many miracles there because of their lack of faith." (Matthew 13:53-58)*

I once knew an elderly couple whose only child was a highly respected wealth advisor for one of the nation's top wealth management firms. Their son had gained an international reputation for helping millionaires become billionaires and, as a result, he was in high demand by some of the nation's wealthiest individuals. Shortly after his parents retired, the son wanted to help his mom and dad with their financial planning. His parents politely declined his offer to help and told him that they were happy with the advice they were getting from the trust officer at their local bank. Confident that he could more than double the return on their investments, the son pushed his parents on the issue. They would not budge and seemed to dig their heels in a little farther. The son relented, disappointed that his parents trusted a relatively unknown advisor more than their own flesh and blood.

Jesus experienced the same type of reaction when he returned to Nazareth and began teaching in the synagogues. The crowds were impressed by his vast knowledge and his teaching style but once they realized that He was Joseph's son, the son of a carpenter, they began to mock him. Because of their lack of faith, Jesus performed few miracles during his stay there. God does not exist for the pleasure of man. Jesus chose not to satisfy the desire of hearts who were unwilling to believe. We exist to bring God pleasure and without faith it is impossible to please Him (Hebrews 11:6).

I sometimes wonder if our unbelief causes us to miss the miracles performed before our very eyes. While most of us profess to be true believers, there's usually a kernel of doubt that drives a wedge between us and God. What would happen if we put our doubt and sinfulness aside and put our complete trust and faith in God?

### MY PRAYER
*God, open my eyes so that I might see the work You are doing right before me. Turn my unbelief to passionate belief so that I can more boldly witness to the miraculous things You are doing every day. I pray for these things in the name of your Son, Jesus Christ. Amen.*

### READ: JOHN 3:16-21

**QUESTION #1:** What is the cause of your unbelief? Do you believe that God might be doing mighty works in your life that have gone unnoticed?

**QUESTION #2:** Do you believe that you have witnessed a miracle from God? Describe the circumstances and outcome.

### CONTEMPLATE

Write about a situation where you offered advice to a loved one who chose not to accept it. How does your situation compare to the reaction Jesus received in Nazareth?

WEEK 4
DAY 5

# PERSISTENT FAITH

*"A Canaanite woman from that vicinity came to him, crying out, "Lord, Son of David, have mercy on me! My daughter is demon-possessed and suffering terribly." Jesus did not answer a word. So his disciples came to him and urged him, "Send her away, for she keeps crying out after us." He answered, "I was sent only to the lost sheep of Israel." The woman came and knelt before him. "Lord, help me!" she said. He replied, "It is not right to take the children's bread and toss it to the dogs." "Yes it is, Lord," she said. "Even the dogs eat the crumbs that fall from their master's table." Then Jesus said to her, "Woman, you have great faith! Your request is granted." And her daughter was healed at that moment." (Matthew 15:22-28)*

When Jesus was first approached by the Canaanite woman, He had just experienced another confrontation with the Pharisees over why His disciples chose not to wash their hands before they ate. Jesus was preparing to travel to a more remote location where he could be alone with His disciples and distance Himself from the large crowds that had been gathering. The woman was desperate for Jesus to remove demons from her daughter. Because the woman was a Gentile, the disciples showed no compassion for this woman and soon became annoyed at her refusal to leave. Jesus recognized this encounter with the Canaanite as a teaching opportunity for His disciples. Jesus admired her persistence but wanted to test the strength of her faith. He appeared to be dismissive, but the woman continued to plead with Him.

You may recall Jesus's earlier encounter with the Centurion. Like the Canaanite woman, the Centurion was not a Jew; however, both of these individuals impressed Jesus with their strong and persistent faith. The woman repeatedly referred to Jesus as the Son of David, showing that she knew what the prophets had said about the return of the Messiah. Jesus wanted his disciples to understand that there would be a place in God's kingdom for Gentiles and anyone else who demonstrated a strong faith and belief in God.

The disciples had much to learn from the Canaanite woman's strong faith and persistence; qualities that impressed Jesus. We all can learn something about the need to be more aware of the opportunities that are presented to us daily. These missed opportunities deny us the opportunity to explore new relationships and serve those whom God has sent our way.

## MY PRAYER

*Heavenly Father, let me be persistent both in my desire to serve You and others. Help me to recognize the beauty and value in the people I encounter in my daily journeys. Let me love them, the way You love me. Help me to set aside my prejudices and see all people as they were made. I pray for these things in the name of your Son, Jesus Christ. Amen.*

### READ: ROMANS 15:9-12

**QUESTION #1:** Recall the first time you met your best friend. What were your initial reactions? What would be missing from your life had you just ignored or dismissed that person?

**QUESTION #2:** Was Jesus referring to the Canaanite woman as a dog? Explain what He meant.

### CONTEMPLATE

Write about the obstacles that prevent you from expanding your network of friends and acquaintances. What are the factors that lead you to be restrictive in allowing relationships to develop?

*"Let the little children come to me, and do not hinder them, for the kingdom of heaven belongs to such as these."*

**(Matthew 19:14 NIV)**

# WEEK 5

**WEEK 5 DAY 1**

# DENYING YOURSELF

*Then Jesus said to his disciples, "Whoever wants to be my disciple must deny themselves and take up their cross and follow me. For whoever wants to save their life will lose it, but whoever loses their life for me will find it. What good will it be for someone to gain the whole world, yet forfeit their soul? Or what can anyone give in exchange for their soul? For the Son of Man is going to come in his Father's glory with his angels, and then he will reward each person according to what they have done. (Matthew 16:24-27)*

---

When I think about the proposition that Jesus put before his disciples, I find myself wondering whether or not I, myself, would have the courage to truly give up everything and follow Him. Jesus makes it pretty clear that following Him will not be anything like a walk in the park. In a moment of complete authenticity, I have to ask myself this question, "What am I afraid of losing?" I've put so much effort and energy into getting to where I am now. Can I really deny myself the rewards that I feel I have coming to me? I have become so entangled in the comforts of this world that I've dulled my ability to fully comprehend the greater rewards that come from living in light of eternity.

With the words, "follow me," Jesus is asking each of us to make a true commitment, with no turning back. For most of us, the prospect of picking up the cross and carrying it, even for a short distance, seems overwhelming. The truth is that doing what we can to advance and improve our physical life has essentially put our rewards in eternity at risk. As much as I love Jesus, I still struggle with selfishness and my innate desire for self-preservation. Most of us lack the perspective that our lives on this earth are temporary at best. Whatever we give up in this world will be rewarded exponentially in the eternal world. To die is to live. To lose is to win.

Jesus wants us to let Him live through us. In Galatians 2:20, we are reminded that we were crucified with Christ but we, nonetheless, live. Christ lives in us through our very faith in the Son of God who gave himself for us. Ultimately, we will only be judged by the treasures we've stored up in heaven. As difficult as it may seem in the present moment, our lives are but a flash in time. Because of God's promise to us, we have an eternal home in heaven. Once we've arrived, however, our works on earth will determine the rewards we get in God's heaven.

### MY PRAYER
*Father, God, I pray for the wisdom to recognize that my life is not my own. Everything I have is because of You. Help me to overcome that which is holding me back from living the full life that will allow me to deny myself and carry the cross which you have asked me to shoulder. I pray for these things in the name of your Son, Jesus Christ. Amen.*

### READ: I CORINTHIANS 3:10-15

**QUESTION #1:** What would "denying yourself" look like in your life?

**QUESTION #2:** What aspects of your physical life would be the most difficult to give up?

### CONTEMPLATE

Write about what you think an eternal life looks like. What are the rewards that you hope to experience in heaven? What are you most looking forward to?

WEEK 5 DAY 2

# RECKLESS LOVE OF GOD

*"What do you think? If a man owns a hundred sheep, and one of them wanders away, will he not leave the ninety-nine on the hills and go to look for the one that wandered off? And if he finds it, truly I tell you, he is happier about that one sheep than about the ninety-nine that did not wander off. In the same way your Father in heaven is not willing that any of these little ones should perish. (Matthew 18:12-14)*

In this parable, Jesus tells of the shepherd who left 99 of his 100 sheep unattended on a hillside while he went to look for the one sheep in his flock that had wandered off. For most of us, the whole idea of leaving the majority of your sheep at risk to look for just one seems rather counter-intuitive. In this parable, the shepherd is God and we are His lost sheep. I suppose that in the grand scheme of things, most of what God does for us is highly unusual, especially by today's standards. God's relentless pursuit of us, no matter how much we've sinned, causes Him to make extraordinary accommodations for us.

God rejoices when men are restored. He takes such delight when someone who has been lost is suddenly found. Similar to the Parable of the Prodigal Son, the Father lavishes an abundance of love on the son who returns after squandering his inheritance on a sinful life. In James 5:19-20, this message is reinforced with these words, "My brothers and sisters, if one of you should wander from the truth and someone should bring that person back, remember this: Whoever turns a sinner from the error of their way will save them from death and cover over a multitude of sins." What's the point? God wants us to be just as excited and encouraging when someone who has strayed away or left the church comes back into the fold.

The enemy's goals are accomplished when one of us gets separated from the crowd. When a man goes into isolation, he is easy prey for Satan. When we don't have other men close by to keep us accountable and engaged, we tend to slide down the slippery slope of sin. The good news is that God is always looking for us, even when we're hiding. The good shepherd will not rest until He has found His lost sheep. As Christians, we have an obligation to keep an eye out for those who are wandering off and turning away from God. We are called to respond to those who stray with grace and truth, always showing our love and concern.

### MY PRAYER

*God, help me to keep watch for those who are struggling and turning away from You. Help me to also recognize when I, myself, am wandering away and moving towards isolation. Let me share Your joy when someone who was once lost is now found. I pray for these things in the name of Your Son, Jesus Christ. Amen.*

### READ: LUKE 15:3-7

**QUESTION #1:** Why do you suppose risking the welfare of 99 sheep to save the one that wandered away is considered counter-intuitive by today's standards?

**QUESTION #2:** What can you do to create a heightened sense of accountability with the men in your circle?

### CONTEMPLATE

Write about a period of time in your life where you might have wandered away from God. What brought you back? How did your life change afterward?

**WEEK 5 — DAY 3**

# CHILDLIKE FAITH

*"Then people brought little children to Jesus for him to place his hands on them and pray for them. But the disciples rebuked them. Jesus said, "Let the little children come to me, and do not hinder them, for the kingdom of heaven belongs to such as these." When he had placed his hands on them, he went on from there." (Matthew 19:13-15)*

Jesus was drawn to the weakness and innocence of small children. Of course, during this time in history, the mortality rate for small children was quite high. It was also common for small children to be sick. When He had the opportunity to embrace these children and bless them, he jumped at the opportunity. At first, the disciples rebuked the parents of these small children for causing a delay in their travels by distracting Jesus. You may recall an earlier passage in the Gospel of Matthew where the disciples rebuked the Canaanite woman for her persistence in wanting to talk with Jesus. Just as He did before, Jesus saw a teaching opportunity for His disciples and intentionally gave the children His full attention.

The children came to Jesus with nothing to offer and nothing to ask of Him. Unlike most of the adults who encountered Jesus, these children had no self-centered interests. They simply wanted an embrace from Jesus with no expectation of a miracle that needed to be performed or any other need. They were unassuming. Jesus welcomed them with open arms. From this the disciples learned that the best way to approach Jesus is with complete humility and faith. It became clear when Jesus said, "the kingdom of heaven belongs to such as these." With these words, Jesus made it known that adults who approached the kingdom

# CHILDLIKE FAITH

of heaven with the same innocence and humility of these children could expect an eternal life with many rewards.

If we want to be used by God, we must recognize our powerlessness. We must go to God with nothing so that He can give us everything. When we are selfless and humble, we can have the greatest impact in our service to God by serving others. Too often, we let our pride and sophistication stand in the way of us creating a true connection with God. Like the small children in this passage, we must not let others get in our way of bonding with Jesus.

## MY PRAYER

*Lord, I come to you with nothing, hoping that You will give me everything. You have selflessly given me your righteousness so that when God the Father sees me, he also sees You. I am so unworthy of this gift but let me spend the rest of my days free of pride and fear, serving others so that they will see You. Take away my trust in my power so that I can approach You as an innocent child. For these things, I pray in the name of Your Son, Jesus Christ. Amen.*

## READ: LUKE 18:17

**QUESTION #1:** How will you free yourself of the pride and selfishness that prevents you from having a childlike relationship with Christ?

**QUESTION #2:** What are your first memories of knowing about Christ as a child?

## CONTEMPLATE

What steps can you take to change the way you approach Christ? What will be the most significant obstacles?

# SERVANT LEADERSHIP

*Jesus called them together and said, "You know that the rulers of the Gentiles lord it over them, and their high officials exercise authority over them. Not so with you. Instead, whoever wants to become great among you must be your servant, and whoever wants to be first must be your slave— just as the Son of Man did not come to be served, but to serve, and to give his life as a ransom for many." (Matthew 20:25-28)*

---

If you study the surrounding verses and the overall context of this passage, you know that the disciples are in a bit of power struggle over which of the 12 disciples are going to be of the greatest importance in God's kingdom. Jesus is not amused by this discussion and quickly gives His disciples a lesson on humility and servant leadership. It's normal for men to be competitive on and off the field, but Jesus quickly surmised that even those in his innermost circle had completely missed a critical point of his teachings. Being an effective and respected leader begins with a belief that all men are essentially equal. Even when the cultural norms seem to put a very high value on status, the best leader to emerge from the pack is always the one who is willing to serve people rather than use them.

A leader with a servant's heart appreciates the true worth of each individual and does not consider himself to be above any job or any person. If the toilet needs to be scrubbed, he's reaching for the Ajax. You can spot a servant leader when he's walking across the parking lot and stops to pick up a piece of litter. He's the last guy to go through the food line at the company picnic. By heavenly standards, a true servant leader is the one who is willing to lay down his life on behalf of his people.

Jesus was like that and He set the standard very high, expecting His disciples to do the very same. Following Jesus was not for the faint of heart.

In John 13:12-15, just before the Feast of the Passover, Jesus put aside his outer garments, filled a basin with water, and began to wash the feet of his disciples. Some protested but Jesus persisted hoping to drive home a very important message to his disciples. He wanted them to understand that no one was exempt from serving others. True leadership is found in serving others. He who shows the most humility and demonstrates his complete unworthiness is the one most worthy of leading. If the Master of the Universe was so willing to deny Himself in the service of others, how much more should be expected of us mere mortals?

## MY PRAYER

*God, make me a faithful servant to You and to all my brothers and sisters. Let me be mindful that putting others first is the very least that You expect from me. I pray for these things in the name of you Son, Jesus Christ. Amen.*

## READ: JOHN 13:1-20

**QUESTION #1:** What specific things could you do in the line of service to others to be more of a servant leader?

**QUESTION #2:** Describe the difference between your best boss ever and your worst boss ever.

## CONTEMPLATE

Write about an experience you had with someone who was a great example of a servant leader.

# RIGHTEOUS INDIGNATION

*Jesus entered the temple courts and drove out all who were buying and selling there. He overturned the tables of the money changers and the benches of those selling doves. "It is written," he said to them, "My house will be called a 'house of prayer,' but you are making it 'a den of robbers.'"*
*(Matthew 21:12-13)*

---

I remember participating in my first Bible Study and hearing my pastor tell the story of Jesus turning over the tables in the temple and chasing out the money changers and vendors. I was very immature in my faith at the time but I recall being surprised that Jesus could become angry. I thought that anger was a sin, which conflicted with my belief that Jesus was the only one among us who had not sinned. When I asked my pastor why Jesus was susceptible to this type of human emotion, he chalked it up to "righteous indignation." I later learned that "righteous indignation" or anger was the only form of anger that is not a sin. When you react angrily to a mistreatment or an injustice toward another person, your compassionate response is not a sin at all. Paul said "Be angry and do not sin" (Ephesians 4:26). Anger is an emotion, but how should we respond to that emotion? Jesus responded in the defense of others and He protected their access to God.

When Gentiles would visit the Temple, they were restricted to a courtyard on the outermost limits of the Temple grounds. It was there that vendors would take advantage of visitors by requiring them to exchange their foreign currencies for a sacred coinage that was required to pay the Temple tax. The exchange rates charged by these money changers were predatory. The same was true for those who were selling doves and other animals that were to be used for Temple sacrifices.

We learn in 1 Kings 7:23-26 that God gave King David the dimensions for His temple with specific instructions on how it should be built. Once David's son, Solomon had completed building the Temple, God consecrated it and put His name on it. Jesus was upset that what was built as a house of prayer for all nations had become a marketplace of sinful behavior and he let his anger be a clear signal of his displeasure. God wants us to become so passionate about the mistreatment and injustice done to others that we stand up and show our displeasure. If we won't stand up to defend the least among us, who will? Sometimes you have to turn over a table or two to get someone's attention. It worked for Jesus and it will work for us.

### MY PRAYER
*God, give me the passion to stand up against evil and all that goes against Your teaching. Let me the defender of those who have been mistreated and the victims of injustice. Let my only anger be that which is extended for those who cannot defend themselves. I pray for these things in the name of your Son, Jesus Christ. Amen.*

### READ: JOHN 2:13-17

**QUESTION #1:** What would you consider to be the modern-day equivalent of selling goods in the Temple courtyard?

**QUESTION #2:** What are the obstacles that keep you from standing up for what is right?

### CONTEMPLATE

Write about a time when you felt compelled to up against the status quo and defend something important. How were you treated as a result? How did you feel once you had done the right thing?

*"Therefore go and make disciples of all nations, baptizing them in the name of the Father and of the Son and of the Holy Spirit, 20 and teaching them to obey everything I have commanded you. And surely I am with you always, to the very end of the age."*

(Matthew 28:19-20 NIV)

# WEEK 6

# PREPARING THE WAY

*"Therefore keep watch, because you do not know on what day your Lord will come. But understand this: If the owner of the house had known at what time of night the thief was coming, he would have kept watch and would not have let his house be broken into. So you also must be ready, because the Son of Man will come at an hour when you do not expect him. (Matthew 24:42-44)*

---

Perhaps it would be helpful to stop and ask ourselves this question, "How would you change your daily life if you knew that Christ was returning next month?" Would you do anything differently today? For many of us, so much time has elapsed since Christ lived and died on this earth that it's hard for us to conceive that his return could be just around the corner. As a result, we lose our sense of urgency to prepare for His return.

It's so easy to get caught up in the hustle and bustle of life. As a result, there are plenty of things that can keep us distracted from working on our relationship with God. If you have children, you probably know that raising them is fraught with challenges. It's a constant battle to protect them from the negative influences of their peers, authority figures, and whatever they see on social media. And there is, of course, the unresolved issues from our families of origin where there is lingering conflict with our siblings or parents. God wants us to rise above these worldly challenges and be faithful and watchful for the return of Jesus.

God desires to see a sense of urgency in our lives with respect to the second coming of Jesus. There should be no difference in how we are living our lives, whether His anticipated return is next week or 300 years from now. Our lives should be filled with good deeds and we should kick our discipleship efforts into high gear. If you knew that Christ was coming next week, wouldn't you want your brother-in-law, co-worker or best friend to be ready for an eternal life with Christ? Why wait? God wants us to be faithful, watchful, and to live with a sense of urgency about the coming of His Kingdom.

### MY PRAYER

*God, help me prepare for the second coming of Christ with a sense of urgency and reverence. Let me take on today what I've been putting off for tomorrow. Give me the courage to bring men to You starting today and never ceasing until Your Kingdom has come. I pray for these things in the name of your Son, Jesus Christ. Amen.*

### READ: 1 THESSALONIANS 4:13-18

**QUESTION #1:** What would you change about your daily routines if you knew that Christ was coming next month?

**QUESTION #2:** What are the things that are making you complacent?

### CONTEMPLATE

Make a list of the men with whom you'd like to encourage to explore a personal relationship with Jesus. What steps will you now take to initiate a conversation about being saved? Who can you enlist to assist you in your discipleship efforts?

# TRUSTING GOD

*Then Jesus went with his disciples to a place called Gethsemane, and he said to them, "Sit here while I go over there and pray." He took Peter and the two sons of Zebedee along with him, and he began to be sorrowful and troubled. Then he said to them, "My soul is overwhelmed with sorrow to the point of death. Stay here and keep watch with me."*
*Going a little farther, he fell with his face to the ground and prayed, "My Father, if it is possible, may this cup be taken from me. Yet not as I will, but as you will." (Matthew 26:36-39)*

---

It's hard to comprehend the intensity of what Jesus must have been feeling in anticipation of the brutal nature of what would be his death by crucifixion. He knew that it was His destiny, but showing us a glimpse of His own humanity, he appealed to God to let Him forgo both the physical pain and the spiritual pain of separation from the Father (2 Corinthians 5:21). As Jesus prayed in that grove of olive trees in the Garden at Gethsemane, he experienced the very human emotions of anguish and anxiety. Because Christ came to the earth in human form, He experienced the pain and suffering that each of us are likely to face at some point in our lives.

Even though Jesus died on that cross, His eternal role as our King and protector did not. We can find comfort in knowing that Jesus has never been separated from us. When we face an uncertain medical diagnosis or the unexpected loss of a loved one, Jesus knows our pain and He understands our feelings of dread. In his darkest moments on this earth, He set an example for all of us to follow by putting his complete trust in God's will. When we accept God's will, He gives us the strength to endure every hardship and setback. The same God who created the valleys also created the mountains; and we can rejoice in knowing that through good times and bad, God has a perfect plan for our lives.

An important step towards accepting God's will is to simply surrender the desire to control of our lives and accept the truth that God uses everything for our good and His glory. When we surrender, God changes us and we become spiritually equipped to handle what He sends our way. Surrender does not mean giving up. We are called to persevere through all of life's challenges so that we can one day see the purpose of God's perfect plan.

## MY PRAYER
*God, I pray for the courage and confidence to surrender to Your will. Give me the wisdom I need to better understand Your character and the good that You have planned for my life. Help me to embrace the trials and to grow spiritually through the highs and lows of my life. I pray for these things in the name of Your Son, Jesus Christ. Amen.*

### READ: HEBREWS 10:32-39

**QUESTION #1:** What steps can you take now to better understand the character of God? What can you do to spend more time in the Word? How will you change your prayer life?

**QUESTION #2:** What will it take for you to put your complete trust in God's will?

### CONTEMPLATE

Recall a trial in your past when you questioned God's motives. Looking back, how did that difficult time affect your life as you know it today?

# THE DEATH OF CHRIST

*And when Jesus had cried out again in a loud voice, he gave up his spirit. At that moment the curtain of the temple was torn in two from top to bottom. The earth shook, the rocks split and the tombs broke open. The bodies of many holy people who had died were raised to life. They came out of the tombs after Jesus' resurrection and went into the holy city and appeared to many people. When the centurion and those with him who were guarding Jesus saw the earthquake and all that had happened, they were terrified, and exclaimed, "Surely he was the Son of God!" (Matthew 27:50-54)*

---

When Christ died on the cross, the world changed in a very dramatic way. At the very moment of His death, the curtain of the temple was torn, an earthquake shook the earth, rocks split, and the saints rose to walk on the earth. If you're a fan of science fiction thrillers, this may sound like something out of a zombie apocalypse movie. Instead, this was God's way of letting mankind know that their sin had just put the Messiah to death. Those left behind knew instantly that Jesus was indeed the Son of God. In spite of what seemed like a tragic turn of events, Jesus' death on the cross was not a defeat for mankind; instead, it was a tremendous victory for man. Our ransom had now been paid. God could now see us as He saw Jesus.

The symbolism in this passage is quite remarkable. Man was no longer separated from God. The torn veil, which once separated the Holy Place from the Most Holy Place, was no longer a barrier between man and God. From that moment forward, all people were now free to approach God directly. Jesus had accomplished what no holy man or prophet had been able to accomplish. People now had direct access to a wonderful and loving God.

Up through the very end, Jesus was still in control, choosing when to take his last breath and then choosing to send his own spirit to be with His Father. There's no doubt that the death of Jesus got the attention of His world. The darkness that set over the land was a sign of God's wrath and the shaking of the earth was nature's own reaction to the death of Jesus. As followers of Christ, we must understand that His death on the cross was as impactful for unbelievers as it was for the faithful. The reaction of the centurion, after witnessing all that took place, acknowledged clearly that Jesus must have been the Son of God, an affirmation that even those with no faith were moved to consider. Jesus gave his life for all sinners, both believers and unbelievers.

### MY PRAYER

*God, help me to absorb the impact of the death of Jesus and how Your sacrifice changed the world for believers and unbelievers. Help me to recognize the depth and breadth of a love so strong that You were willing to give up Your only Son. Let these facts make me steadfast in my walk. I pray for these things in the name of Your Son, Jesus Christ. Amen.*

### READ: GALATIANS 2:19-21

**QUESTION #1:** In what ways did the death of Christ solidify God's relationship with man?

**QUESTION #2:** What is the one detail surrounding Christ's death that you find most compelling?

### CONTEMPLATE

How do the details associated with Christ's death affect your spiritual status? Write about the emotions you felt while reading of this account.

WEEK 6 DAY 4

# CHRIST IS RISEN

*The angel said to the women, "Do not be afraid, for I know that you are looking for Jesus, who was crucified. He is not here; he has risen, just as he said. Come and see the place where he lay. Then go quickly and tell his disciples: 'He has risen from the dead and is going ahead of you into Galilee. There you will see him.' Now I have told you." (Matthew 28:5-7)*

---

On the day of Christ's resurrection, Mary Magdalene and Mary, the mother of James, went to visit the tomb where Jesus' body had been laid to rest two days earlier. They were stunned to find it empty and to encounter an angel, who told them to go and spread the good news and to tell the disciples that Jesus would meet them in Galilee. On that day, Jesus rose from the dead and, in doing so, accomplished all that he had promised. Thankfully, death was not the end for Jesus and nor will it be for us. In his dying and resurrection, Jesus validated everything He had promised about eternal life and, in turn, gave all of us a new beginning.

You may find it interesting that Jesus's disciples were not the first to learn that He had indeed risen from the dead. Based on the prophecy and the teachings Jesus had shared with them, you would have expected his remaining 11 followers to be waiting by the tomb at the crack of dawn on the third day. Not the case. In the final days of His life, His disciples had denied him, betrayed him, and abandoned him. Now, many days after his crucifixion, some of His disciples had already stopped fishing for men and had returned to fishing for fish. In spite of this, Jesus wanted to greet his disciples in Galilee. That's the beautiful thing about our Savior. He accepts us as we are, flawed and broken. He looks forward to the day that we are reunited with Him.

Jesus has chosen to use our brokenness as part of His mission. In spite of our deficiencies, He wants us to represent Him. We now have the hope that the same power that brought Jesus back to life can somehow restore us and bring our spiritual selves to life. We need to be rescued from our sin so we can begin to live our lives following the example that Christ established for us. In what ways are you living according to your new life in Christ? God fulfilled a major promise that had been made to us. Jesus wiped away our sin through His suffering on the cross. What else do we need to know to start anew?

## MY PRAYER

*Jesus, by Your death and resurrection, You gave me a new beginning. Let me dedicate myself to making sure that my new life reflects the life you led while on this earth. Let me be steadfast in my desire to serve and to make the most of all that You've given me. For these things, I pray in Your name, the Son of God, my Savior. Amen.*

### READ: 1 CORINTHIANS 15:42-58

**QUESTION #1:** Why do you believe that Jesus was tolerant of the misdeeds of His disciples during the final days of His life? What lesson can we learn from this?

**QUESTION #2:** Do you believe that Jesus Christ can fully accept your flaws and brokenness? Why or why not?

### CONTEMPLATE

Write a prayer asking God to renew your life so that you might walk in that newness of life. Ask God to take away the barriers that keep you from fully enjoying your fellowship with Him.

# GO. BAPTIZE. TEACH.

*Then the eleven disciples went to Galilee, to the mountain where Jesus had told them to go. When they saw him, they worshiped him; but some doubted. Then Jesus came to them and said, "All authority in heaven and on earth has been given to me. Therefore go and make disciples of all nations, baptizing them in the name of the Father and of the Son and of the Holy Spirit, and teaching them to obey everything I have commanded you. And surely I am with you always, to the very end of the age." (Matthew 28:16-20 NIV)*

---

The details surrounding the death, burial, and resurrection of Christ may be perhaps the most important words that come to us from the Gospel of Matthew. When the 11 remaining disciples were called to Galilee, the place where Jesus' ministry first began, they encounter Jesus on the mountain where they would receive instructions now known as the Great Commission.

On that mountain, Jesus gave his disciples His final commandment. Their mission was to go out to every nation and make disciples. It was noteworthy that they were now being instructed to reach out not just to Jews, but to all people. The 11 were instructed to baptize their new converts as a first step in making disciples. The act of baptism was an important aspect of their mission because the act, itself, symbolized one's submission to Christ and an obedience that came from faith. Teaching others about obeying Christ and about His good news was an essential part of the Great Commission. The more one knows about God and His character, the more effective they can be in helping others know God. And the disciples were instructed to 'go' and make disciples as they lived out their lives and mission.

# GO. BAPTIZE. TEACH.

Jesus taught His disciples to baptize in the name of the Father, the Son, and the Holy Spirit. At that moment, Jesus made a promise that would give His disciples the encouragement they would need to forge ahead. The presence of Jesus would always be with them through the Holy Spirit who would provide them with wisdom, understanding, counsel, fortitude, knowledge, piety, and a fear of the Lord. Through the Holy Spirit, all of us experience the presence of God on this earth and in all that we do. Though Jesus would soon ascend into heaven, the Holy Spirit would be with the disciples for all times.

## MY PRAYER

*God, let me find comfort and strength in the promise you gave us through the Great Commission. Let me find new opportunities every day to go and make disciples, baptize them, and teach the good news found in Your Word. May I do all of this with the confidence of knowing the Holy Spirit is present in all that I do. I pray for these things in the name of Your Son, Jesus Christ. Amen.*

### READ: JOHN 1:9-13

**QUESTION #1:** Were you baptized? If so, what does your baptism mean to you?

**QUESTION #2:** Do you feel equipped to teach others about the good news of Christ? What steps can you take to better prepare yourself?

### CONTEMPLATE

Describe your relationship with the Holy Spirit. In what ways do you feel the presence of Jesus when you lean into the spirit? How can make yourself more aware and engaged in the works of the Holy Spirit?

# EPILOGUE

## MARCHING ORDERS

*Then Jesus came to them and said, "All authority in heaven and on earth has been given to me. Therefore go and make disciples of all nations, baptizing them in the name of the Father and of the Son and of the Holy Spirit, and teaching them to obey everything I have commanded you." (Matthew 28:18-19)*

The wisdom that comes from the Gospel of Matthew can be life-changing if you're willing to set aside your woundedness and surrender to the indisputable fact that God's promises are indeed true. Give yourself permission to embrace this timeless truth, accept His love, and then pay it forward by extending His love to others.

Your next move is to share this good news. Begin by asking God to prepare the hearts and minds of the people you know who would benefit from having a personal relationship with Christ. Remember that your first step as a disciple of Christ is to live a life that simply demonstrates your love for others. You can spread the love of Christ by your actions, without having to say a single word.

The absolute truth is that God will always be with you and protect you. He will be your strength and He will provide for you. He'll answer your prayers and give you peace in what might be your darkest hours. Most importantly, God will ALWAYS love you… even when you feel unworthy. Take comfort in knowing that He has already sent his Son to cover your sins. Your ransom has been paid. What an awesome gift from a loving Father.

Thank you for reading this book. I hope you'll consider passing it on to someone whose life might be changed by hearing of God's good news through simply walking with Matthew.

Go forth and make disciples.

Fred Parry

## ADDITIONAL RESOURCES

Becoming The Man God Intended You To Be

Interested in using this book for a small group or Bible Study? Visit our website for FREE study materials, discussion questions, handouts, rules of engagement for small group participants, and other teaching tools.

Looking for a speaker for your next men's event?

Contact Fred Parry,
711 West Broadway, Columbia, Missouri 65203
or email fparry61@gmail.com

www.FredParry.Life

## DISCOVER THE FULL SERIES

# Walking With The Saints

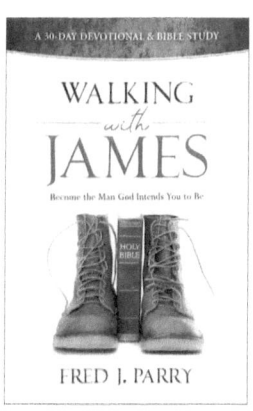
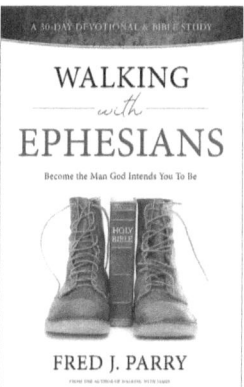
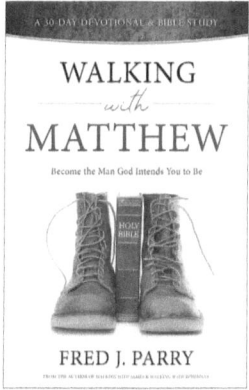

Now available in eBook
and Paperback on Amazon

www.FredParry.Life

www.ingramcontent.com/pod-product-compliance
Lightning Source LLC
Chambersburg PA
CBHW022019290426
44109CB00015B/1240